Sell your Brand

Evelyn Wright

Evelyn Wright

Copyright Page

Index

What is a Brand and Why is it Important?   7
Building the Foundations of Your Brand   12
The Power of Brand Design   18
The Meaning Behind Your Logo   24
The Language of your Brand   30
Define your Ideal Audience   37
Make your Brand Viral   44
How to Create an Experience that Makes You Fall in Love   52
The Power of Storytelling in your Brand   60
Humanizing your Personal Brand   68
From Local to Global   76
Collaborations and Brand Ambassadors   84
Measuring and Optimizing Your Brand's Success   92
Make People Love Buying Your Brand   100

Evelyn Wright

Evelyn Wright

What is a Brand and Why is it Important?

A brand is much more than a name or a logo. It is the way people perceive a product, a service, or even a person. It is the mental image that forms in the minds of consumers every time they hear about a company or a professional. A brand is the sum of everything a company stands for: its identity, its values, what it promises to customers, and how those customers feel when interacting with it. Simply put, a brand is the emotional connection established between an entity and its audience. That is why it is so important to understand that building a strong brand is not just about creating a good design, but about achieving a genuine and lasting relationship with the public.

The importance of a brand lies in the fact that it is what differentiates a company or person from their competitors. In a market saturated with options, having a clear and defined brand allows the public to recognize you, remember you, and most importantly, choose you over other options. It doesn't matter if you are selling a high-tech product or simply offering a basic service, what really stands out is how you make people feel when they think of you or what you offer. A strong brand not only generates sales, but it creates loyalty, and that is what every company or professional wants: clients who come back again and again.

A brand is also important because it conveys trust. Consumers tend to choose brands they trust, and that trust isn't built overnight. It takes time, consistency, and authenticity. Every interaction customers have with your brand, whether it's through a purchase, a social media post, or simply seeing your logo, contributes to that trust. When a brand is consistent and delivers on its promises, customers begin to associate it with trustworthiness, and that's key to long-term success.

Another vital aspect of a brand is its ability to tell a story. People don't just buy products or services, they buy stories, they buy experiences. Think about the most recognizable brands in the world: each one tells a story that connects emotionally with its audience. Whether it's the story of a small family business growing from strength to strength into a giant or the promise of delivering the most innovative product, a good story makes a brand much more than just a material thing. It makes people feel like they're part of something bigger.

Furthermore, a brand is a reflection of the values you stand for. Today, more than ever, consumers are aware of what lies behind a brand. They want to know that the companies they associate with share their principles and values. It is no longer enough to offer a good product; people want the brands they trust to be ethical, responsible and do good. So when building a brand, it is essential that you think about the values you want to convey, as these will be a fundamental part of how people perceive and value your offering.

Finally, a brand is important because it has the power to influence. A strong brand can change the way people think, feel and act. It can make people make decisions based on emotions and not just logic. For example, a person might be willing to pay more for a product from a brand they trust, even if there are cheaper options on the market. That's the magic of a well-built brand: it can create such a deep impact on people that sometimes they're not just buying a product, they're buying a feeling, a lifestyle, an identity.

In short, a brand is the emotional representation of everything a company or person is. It's how others see you and how you choose to present yourself to the world. And it's important because it defines who you are, what you do, and how you connect with your audience.

Building the Foundations of Your Brand

Building a brand foundation is the first step to getting people to recognize you, trust you, and ultimately choose you. Before you think about logos, colors, or advertising campaigns, it's essential that you take the time to define the foundation that will hold everything else together. This means asking yourself who you are, what you offer, and why what you do matters. This process may seem somewhat abstract at first, but it's what will give your brand a strong, coherent identity that people can recognize and understand.

The first thing you need to be clear about is the values you want your brand to represent. Values are the core beliefs that will guide all the decisions you make from now on. These values can be things like honesty, innovation, quality, sustainability, or any other principle you consider essential. Think of values as the heart of your brand, what makes it different from all the others and what gives meaning to what you offer. If your brand doesn't have well-defined values, it will be difficult to connect with people in an authentic and meaningful way. That's why it's vital that you take the time to define what really matters to you and how that is reflected in your brand.

Once you have your values nailed down, it's time to define your brand's mission. Your mission is basically the reason your brand exists. Why do you do what you do? What problem are you solving for your customers? What change do you want to see in the world through your brand? This mission should be clear, simple, and easy to understand for anyone who comes across your brand. It doesn't have to be overly complicated or grandiose—it just has to be authentic. For example, if you have a personal care brand, your mission could be "to provide natural products that help people care for their skin in a healthy way without harsh chemicals." The important thing is that this mission is something that both you and your audience can relate to.

The next step in building the foundation of your brand is to define your value proposition. This is where you really start to shape what you offer. The value proposition is what differentiates your brand from others that offer similar products or services. It's the answer to the question: why should someone choose you over the competition? To define it, it's helpful to think about what you do better than anyone else. Maybe your products are more affordable, higher quality, or made with unique ingredients. Or maybe what you offer is a customer experience that no one else can match. Whatever it is, it should be clear what it is that your brand brings to the table that others can't. That will be the main reason people will choose you.

A key part of this foundation is knowing your audience. You can't build a strong brand if you don't know who you're building for. Who is your target audience? What do they need? What are their concerns, desires, and expectations? Understanding your audience is key because it will allow you to design a brand that speaks directly to them. If you try to reach everyone, you're very likely to reach no one. You need to be specific in your approach. If your audience is young people interested in sustainable fashion, your design decisions, tone of voice, and messaging will be very different than a brand that targets entrepreneurs looking for innovative technology. Knowing your audience will allow you to connect in a deeper, more authentic way.

It's also important to consider consistency as one of the pillars of your brand. Consistency means that every aspect of your brand should be aligned with the values, mission, and value proposition you've defined. This includes everything from your logo design and color choices to the way you communicate with customers on social media or customer service. If your brand promises something, it should deliver on that promise in every interaction you have with your audience. Consistency is what builds trust and credibility, two essential elements for any brand's success. If your brand is consistent at all times, people will know what to expect from you and can trust that you will deliver what you promise.

Finally, don't forget that the foundations of a brand are not static. While it's important to have strong values, mission, and value proposition, you must also be flexible and willing to adapt when necessary. Markets change, trends evolve, and customer needs can change over time. Your brand must be prepared to evolve with them. This doesn't mean you have to change your core principles, but you do have to be open to adjusting certain aspects to stay relevant and connected to your audience. The ability to adapt is what will make your brand last over time.

In short, building the foundations of your brand is an essential process that defines who you are, what you do, and how you relate to your audience. By having clear values, a defined mission, a unique value proposition, and a consistent approach, you will be on the right path to creating a strong brand that will stand the test of time and genuinely connect with people.

The Power of Brand Design

Brand design is one of the most powerful tools you have to communicate who you are and what you offer, without the need for words. It is the first contact that most people will have with your brand, and although it can often seem superficial, design is capable of transmitting very profound messages in a matter of seconds. A good brand design can be the difference between capturing someone's attention or going unnoticed. And it's not just about making something that is visually appealing; it's about designing something that clearly and effectively represents what your brand wants to convey.

When we talk about brand design, we're talking about many elements that together create a coherent and recognizable image. The most obvious is the logo, but there are also colors, fonts, images, and even the way you organize information on your products or advertising. All of these elements combine to create a unique visual identity that should reflect the essence of your brand. An effective design not only makes people remember your brand, but it also transmits a series of emotions and sensations that lead them to connect with you more deeply.

The power of brand design is that it can communicate a complex idea quickly and easily. For example, the colors you choose for your brand have a direct impact on how people perceive it. Colors aren't just pleasing to the eye; they also evoke emotions. Blue, for example, is often associated with trust and professionalism. That's why so many companies in the financial or technology sector use it. Red, on the other hand, is a color that conveys energy, passion, and urgency, which is why we see it in brands that want to attract attention quickly, such as fast food brands. Choosing the right colors for your brand isn't just a matter of aesthetics, but a strategic decision that directly influences how others perceive you.

Another key aspect of brand design is the logo. This little symbol or set of words is often the most direct visual representation of who you are. A good logo should be simple, memorable, and most importantly, representative of your brand. It doesn't have to be complicated or extremely detailed – in fact, some of the most effective and recognizable logos in the world are incredibly simple. Think of the logos of big brands like Nike or Apple. They're simple, but they pack a huge punch because they perfectly represent the identity of those brands. A good logo is easy to remember and helps people quickly recognize you.

In addition to the logo and colors, the typeface you choose also plays an important role in your brand design. Just like with colors, different typefaces can convey different feelings. Serif typefaces, which have small details in the letters, are often seen as traditional and reliable, while sans-serif typefaces, which are cleaner and more modern, are perceived as fresh and simple. Choosing the right typeface can make your messages clearer and reinforce your brand's personality. That's why big brands take care of every detail, even the font they use on their products or advertisements.

Brand design is also about consistency. It doesn't matter how good the individual elements of your design are if they aren't well-coordinated and presented consistently across all touchpoints with your audience. From your website and social media to your product packaging, everything should follow a single visual line that reinforces your brand identity. Consistency in design is key to creating a strong, trustworthy brand image. If people see one thing on your website, something different on your social media, and something completely different on your products, it will create confusion and you'll miss the opportunity to create a clear, strong connection.

A powerful brand design also has the potential to make people feel like they are part of something bigger. Think of brands that have a loyal following, almost like a community. Often times, that loyalty is built through a visual identity that consumers adopt as part of their own lifestyle. Fashion, technology, or even food brands have achieved this thanks to a brand design that is not only attractive, but also creates a sense of belonging. This happens when your brand design is able to effectively communicate who you are and what you stand for, allowing people to feel connected to those values and want to be a part of what you offer.

Brand design can also be a tool to tell your story. Every element of your design can be a piece of your brand narrative. From colors to logo, everything can have a meaning that reinforces the message you want to convey. For example, if your brand has an eco-focus, you can use colors and visuals that reference nature, which will help people associate your brand with sustainability. In this way, the design becomes an extension of the story you are telling, and helps create a stronger emotional connection with your audience.

In conclusion, the power of brand design goes far beyond what meets the eye. It's not just about creating something pretty, but about designing a visual identity that effectively communicates who you are, what you do, and how you want people to perceive you. From colors to logo and typography, every detail of the design is an opportunity to strengthen your brand and emotionally connect with your audience. A well-thought-out design will not only make people remember you, but it will also inspire them to trust you and be a part of what you offer.

The Meaning Behind Your Logo

Your logo is one of the most important elements of your brand. Although it may look like just a symbol or a set of letters, its meaning goes far beyond the visual. Your logo is, in many cases, the first impression people will have of your brand, and it's what will help them remember you every time they see it. It's like the face of your brand, and what you manage to convey with it will directly influence how people perceive you. A good logo is not only aesthetically pleasing, but it also tells a story, expresses your brand's values, and connects emotionally with your audience.

Every element of a logo has a meaning behind it. From the shape to the colors, everything is there to communicate something specific. For example, rounded shapes in a logo can convey softness, harmony, and approachability, while angular shapes are often associated with strength, stability, or precision. The interesting thing about logo design is that even though it is simple, it has the power to communicate complex ideas in a matter of seconds. People, even if they don't consciously notice it, pick up on these messages when they see a logo and form an immediate impression about the brand it represents.

Color is one of the most powerful aspects of the meaning behind a logo. Colors have the ability to evoke emotions and generate associations. That's why it's essential that you choose your logo colors carefully, thinking about what you want people to feel when they see your brand. Warm tones like red or orange can convey energy, passion, or urgency, while cool tones like blue or green evoke calm, confidence, or serenity. A black and white logo can convey a sense of elegance, simplicity, or professionalism. Each color has its own visual language and contributes to the way your brand is perceived.

Besides color, the typeface you choose for your logo also has a deeper meaning. Using a typeface with elegant, delicate strokes is not the same as using a modern, minimalist typeface. Letters with soft curves often give a more friendly and approachable impression, while letters with right angles and hard lines can communicate strength or formality. For example, luxury brands often use more refined and stylized typefaces, while tech brands often prefer clean, unadorned typefaces, which convey innovation and modernity. It's amazing how, without the need for words, a simple choice of typeface can completely change the tone of your brand.

Another important aspect of logo design is symmetry. Symmetrical logos, those that are visually balanced, tend to convey a sense of stability, order, and confidence. Asymmetrical logos, on the other hand, can convey dynamism, creativity, or a more casual attitude. The symmetry or asymmetry of your logo also communicates something about your brand's personality. A perfectly balanced logo can say that your brand is trustworthy and solid, while a more unstructured logo can show that your brand is original, innovative, or willing to break with established norms.

Minimalism is another trend in logo design that has a lot of meaning. A minimalist logo, with few elements and simple shapes, usually conveys clarity, modernity, and professionalism. These types of logos work well in an age where people are exposed to an overwhelming amount of information and visual messages. A simple and straightforward logo can stand out from the noise and be easier to remember. However, even though a minimalist logo may seem simple at first glance, that doesn't mean it's easy to design. It requires a lot of attention to detail and how each element relates to the message you want to convey.

Aside from the visual aspect, your logo can also have an emotional meaning. People tend to form emotional bonds with brands that are familiar to them or that give them a sense of belonging. That's why it's important that your logo design reflects your brand's values and personality. If your brand cares about the well-being of the environment, for example, you might use green colors or shapes reminiscent of nature, which will help create an emotional connection with people who share those same values. When your logo authentically reflects who you are, it's easier for your audience to identify with it and develop loyalty to your brand.

Logos also have the ability to evolve over time. Many brands start with a logo that represents their original vision, but as they grow and change, the logo can also adapt to reflect those new goals. This evolution doesn't mean you have to completely change your logo, but small tweaks can keep it fresh and relevant, without losing its essence. Think of brands that have gone through several versions of their logo, but are still recognizable to their audience. These updates are often subtle, but they reflect the brand's ability to adapt to new trends and needs while staying true to its roots.

In short, the meaning behind a logo goes far beyond what meets the eye. Every shape, color, typeface, and detail is designed to convey a message and connect with your audience visually and emotionally. A good logo is not only memorable, but it also faithfully represents your brand's values, personality, and mission. It is a powerful tool that, when strategically designed, has the potential to leave a lasting impression on people's minds and effectively communicate who you are and what you offer.

The Language of your Brand

Your brand language is how you communicate with the world. It's not just about the words you choose, but the tone, style, and how those words reflect your brand's personality. Just as visual design is essential to capturing attention, the language you use is what will help create a deeper connection with your audience. It's your brand's voice, and that voice should be consistent and authentic across all touchpoints, whether it's on your website, social media, emails, or any other form of communication.

The first step in defining your brand language is to understand your brand personality. Ask yourself how you want people to perceive your brand. Is it friendly and approachable? Is it professional and serious? Is it creative and modern? Your brand personality should be aligned with the values and mission you've previously defined. If, for example, your brand is focused on offering innovative technological solutions, you'll likely want a more professional and direct tone, while if you're targeting a young, creative audience, you can afford to be more casual and fun. The key is that the language you choose accurately reflects who you are and how you want people to relate to you.

Once you have your brand personality figured out, it's important to define the tone you'll use in all of your communications. Tone is the nuance you give to words and how you make your message sound. The same message can be conveyed in different ways depending on the tone you use. For example, if you sell wellness products, you might choose a calm and encouraging tone that inspires trust and reassurance. On the other hand, if your brand is related to fashion or technology, you might want to use a more dynamic and energetic tone that reflects innovation and trends. The right tone helps people identify with your brand and perceive consistency in everything you do.

In addition to tone, writing style is another key aspect of your brand language. Some brands choose a more formal and structured style, while others prefer a more conversational and relaxed style. For example, a brand that targets high-level executives may use a more technical and precise style, with formal language that conveys authority. In contrast, a brand targeting a younger audience might prefer a more casual style, using simple words and expressions that sound natural and relatable. Defining your brand style will allow you to communicate consistently and ensure that your message always comes across in the right way.

Your brand language should also be aligned with the type of audience you're targeting. Speaking to experienced professionals in a specific sector is not the same as speaking to people who are just starting to learn about a product or service. That's why it's essential to know your audience well in order to know what type of language will resonate best with them. If your audience is more technical, they'll likely appreciate more specialized language, while if you're targeting a more general audience, it's important to use words that are more accessible and easy to understand. This will help your messages be clear and effective, regardless of your audience's level of knowledge.

Another important aspect of your brand language is consistency. It is crucial that you maintain the same style and tone across all your communications, no matter what channel you are communicating on. If you use a friendly and approachable tone on your social media, but adopt a distant and formal tone on your website, you will create confusion for your audience. Consistency in language creates trust, as people know what to expect from you at all times. This consistency also reinforces your brand identity, making it easier to recognize and remember. Every word you choose should be in line with the image you want to project and the experience you want to offer.

Your brand language is not only limited to how you communicate directly with your audience, but also how you talk about your products or services. The way you describe what you offer should be clear, but it should also convey the value of what you are selling. Here, it is important to avoid overusing technical jargon or complicated words that can alienate your audience. Your goal is for people to understand exactly what you do and why it is valuable to them. Clear, direct language that focuses on the benefits you offer is key to capturing the attention of your potential customers and motivating them to take action.

Additionally, it's essential that your brand's language has an emotional component. People don't just buy products or services; they buy emotions, experiences, and solutions to their problems. By using language that appeals to your audience's emotions, you'll be building a deeper connection with them. For example, if your brand sells eco-friendly products, you can use language that talks about the importance of caring for the planet and how your product helps them be part of that change. By connecting with your audience's emotions, you'll get them to identify more with your brand and feel more inclined to support it.

Language also has the power to tell a story. A brand that tells a story in an authentic and engaging way is more likely to capture the attention of its audience and make a lasting impact. Your brand story can include why you decided to found your brand, what challenges you've overcome, or what inspires you to do what you do. By using language to tell your story, you're not only humanizing your brand, but you're also creating an emotional bond with the people who follow you. Stories are one of the most effective forms of communication, and when you manage to tell a good story, people are more likely to feel connected to your brand on a personal level.

In short, your brand language is an essential part of your identity. It's not just how you communicate, but also how you build relationships, convey emotions, and tell your story. A well-defined and consistent language will allow you to create a deeper connection with your audience, increase trust in your brand, and make people identify with you. From tone to style to word choice, everything should be aligned with your brand's personality and the values you want to convey. By taking care of your brand language, you'll be creating a unique and recognizable voice that will help you stand out in a competitive market.

Define your Ideal Audience

Defining your ideal audience is one of the most important steps when building your brand. You can't effectively sell a product or service if you don't know exactly who you're talking to. Brands often make the mistake of trying to target everyone, thinking that this will give them more sales opportunities. But in reality, it's much more effective to focus on a specific group of people who really need what you offer and who will be more inclined to buy it. This group is your ideal audience, and when you define them correctly, your marketing and sales efforts become much more efficient.

The first step in defining your ideal audience is to think about who the people are who would benefit the most from what you offer. This means having a clear idea of what kind of problem your product or service solves and what kind of person is most interested in solving that problem. For example, if your brand sells eco-friendly beauty products, your ideal audience is likely made up of people who care about the environment, value personal well-being, and are looking for natural and sustainable products. These people are more willing to pay for products that align with their values and lifestyle.

Once you have a general idea of who your ideal audience might be, it's important to dig deeper into their characteristics. This is known as creating a profile or "buyer persona," which is a detailed description of your ideal customer. This profile should include data such as age, gender, where they live, their educational and professional level, as well as their interests, values, and needs. For example, if your product is targeted at young mothers looking for comfortable and functional clothing for their children, you should consider their daily routine, the challenges they face, and what they value most in the brands they buy. The clearer you are about the profile of your ideal audience, the better you can tailor your message to resonate with them.

In addition to demographics, it's important to understand your ideal audience's behavior. Where do they spend their time online? What type of content do they consume? What are their favorite social networks? These questions will help you know where to find them and how to speak to them effectively. If your ideal audience spends a lot of time on Instagram, your marketing strategy may need to include a strong presence on that platform, with engaging images and videos that capture their attention. On the other hand, if your ideal audience prefers reading blogs or watching informative videos on YouTube, then you should focus your efforts on creating content that provides value to them in those spaces.

Understanding your audience's motivations is also key. What drives them to purchase a product or service? Some may be motivated by price, while others may be more interested in quality or the experience the brand offers them. If you know what your audience values most, you can highlight those aspects in your marketing message and make your offer more appealing to them. For example, if your ideal audience values sustainability, be sure to highlight how your products are made with eco-friendly materials or how your company is committed to responsible practices. By connecting with what they really care about, they are more likely to identify with your brand and choose to buy from you instead of the competition.

Another way to better define your ideal audience is to think about the challenges and problems they face in their everyday lives. Most people are looking for products or services that help them solve some kind of problem or improve their life in some way. For example, if your brand sells productivity tools, your ideal audience might be busy professionals who need to better organize their time and be more efficient at work. If you understand these problems, you can tailor your message to show how your product or service is the perfect solution for them. By speaking directly to their concerns and offering a clear solution, you'll be capturing their attention more effectively.

You should not forget that your ideal audience can also change or evolve over time. As your brand grows and develops, you may find that you attract different types of customers or that your offer starts to resonate with new groups of people. That's why it's important to review and adjust your ideal audience profile periodically, to make sure you're always aligned with the people who are most likely to buy your product. Keep an eye on feedback from your current customers, analyze market trends, and constantly evaluate whether your audience remains the same or whether you need to adjust your strategy to reach new groups.

Defining your ideal audience will not only help you sell more, but it will also allow you to create a more authentic connection with people. When you understand your audience, you can speak to them in a way that is close and personal to them. Instead of blasting out a generic message that might go unnoticed, you'll be speaking directly to the people who matter most to you, using language and an approach that resonates with them. This creates a stronger, longer-lasting relationship between your brand and your audience, which can translate into loyal customers and brand ambassadors in the long run.

Once you're clear on who your ideal audience is, you can tailor every aspect of your brand to align with their expectations and desires. From the design of your product to the way you present your messaging, everything should be designed to capture their attention and meet their needs. For example, if your ideal audience values simplicity, make sure your website is easy to navigate and your purchasing process is as seamless as possible. If they care about personalization, consider offering options so they can tailor your products to their preferences. By tailoring your offering to what truly matters to your audience, you'll be creating a more satisfying experience for them and increasing the likelihood of success for your brand.

In short, defining your ideal audience is a fundamental step in building a successful brand. It's not just about knowing who you're selling to, but deeply understanding their needs, desires, and behaviors. By creating a detailed profile of your ideal customer, you'll be able to tailor your marketing and sales strategies to more effectively connect with the people who are most interested in what you offer. Not only will this connection help you sell more, but it will also allow you to build a more authentic and lasting relationship with your audience, which is key to the long-term success of your brand.

Make your Brand Viral

Making your brand go viral is one of the biggest dreams of any business or entrepreneur. Virality is when a piece of content or an idea spreads quickly among many people, generating enormous exposure in a very short time. However, virality does not happen by accident; although it sometimes seems spontaneous, many brands manage to go viral through well-planned strategies and a deep understanding of what captures the public's attention. Making your brand go viral is not easy, but there are several steps you can take to increase the chances of more people talking about your brand and sharing it massively.

The first step to making your brand go viral is to create content that is highly shareable. This means that the content must be interesting, entertaining, or useful enough that people feel the need to share it with their friends and followers. Shareable content can be of many types: a funny video, an informative infographic, an inspiring article, or even a meme. The important thing is that your content resonates with your audience and generates some kind of emotion in them, whether it's laughter, surprise, empathy, or even curiosity. If the content generates an emotional reaction, people are more likely to want to share it, and that's what can start the process of going viral.

Additionally, for your content to be shareable, it needs to be visually appealing. Nowadays, people consume large amounts of information visually, especially on social media platforms like Instagram, TikTok, and Facebook. Content that includes images, graphics, or videos is much more likely to be shared than content that only contains text. Even if you are sharing an important or informative message, it is advisable to accompany it with an attractive design or images that grab attention from the first moment. If you can get people to stop and look at your content, you will be one step closer to having them share it with others.

Another key aspect of making your brand go viral is to leverage the power of social media. Social media is the ideal place for content to spread quickly and efficiently. Platforms like Instagram, Twitter, Facebook, and TikTok have the ability to amplify your message and get it in front of thousands or even millions of people in a short amount of time. To get the most out of social media, it's important that you post content consistently and engage with your audience. Respond to comments, share stories behind your brand, and participate in relevant conversations within your niche. The more visibility you achieve on social media, the more likely your brand will go viral.

An effective strategy to increase virality is to collaborate with influencers or people who already have a large audience on social media. Influencers have the ability to make your brand reach more people, as they have followers who trust their recommendations and content. By working with an influencer who aligns with your brand values, you can gain greater exposure in an authentic and trustworthy way. Influencers can help you create content, make mentions of your brand, or even participate in more elaborate campaigns that capture the attention of their audience. By partnering with the right people, you can greatly increase the chances of your brand going viral.

Another way to make your brand go viral is to create marketing campaigns that encourage audience participation. Contests, challenges, or giveaways are effective ways to motivate people to engage with your brand and share it with others. For example, you can run a contest where participants must share a photo using your product or create a TikTok challenge that involves users dancing or acting in a way that relates to your brand. By offering a prize or recognition, people will be more willing to participate and share the content, increasing the chances of it being widely spread. These types of campaigns not only help drive virality, but they also foster a deeper connection with your audience.

Storytelling can also be a powerful tool to make your brand go viral. People love good stories, especially those that are emotional, inspiring, or surprising. If you can tell your brand's story in a way that touches people's emotions, they're more likely to share that story with others. For example, you could tell the story of how your brand was born, the challenges you faced along the way, or how your product or service has positively impacted someone's life. By connecting emotionally with your audience, you'll not only be generating more interest in your brand, but you'll also be creating content that people will want to share because it makes them feel something.

Timing is also a key factor in making your brand go viral. Sometimes, viral success is all about being in the right place at the right time. This can mean taking advantage of a current trend or jumping on board a conversation that's already happening on social media. For example, if there's a popular topic that's circulating online and your brand can relate to it in some way, you can join that conversation and increase the chances of your content being shared. Keeping an eye on what's happening in the digital world and knowing when to jump in with relevant content can be a great way to grab attention and get your brand spread.

Additionally, if you want your brand to go viral, you need to make sure that your content is easy to share. This means that your content should be available in the right formats for each platform and that people can share it with just one click. Adding "share" buttons on your website, making it easy to download images or videos, and making sure your content is optimized for mobile devices are some of the ways you can make it easier for your audience to spread the word about your brand. The easier it is for people to share your content, the more likely it is to go viral.

Finally, authenticity is key to virality. People are becoming more aware and critical of what they consume online, and they can easily tell when something seems forced or not genuine. If you want your brand to go viral, it's important that the content you create and the stories you tell are authentic and aligned with your brand values. Don't try to copy what other brands are doing or follow formulas that don't feel natural to you. Instead, focus on showing the true essence of your brand and connecting with your audience in an honest way. Authenticity will not only make your content more valuable, but it will also increase the likelihood that people will share it because they feel it's real and meaningful.

In short, making your brand go viral is no easy feat, but with a well-thought-out strategy and a clear understanding of your audience, it is possible to achieve it. Create shareable content, leverage social media, collaborate with influencers, use the power of stories, and make sure your brand is shareable. Virality may seem unpredictable, but by following these steps and being authentic in everything you do, you will increase your chances of your brand spreading widely and capturing the attention of a large audience.

How to Create an Experience that Makes You Fall in Love

Creating an experience that your customers love is essential to the success of any brand. It's not just about offering a good product or service, but about building an emotional connection with the people who interact with your brand. Experiences that make people love are those that go beyond satisfying a need or solving a problem; they are those that touch the heart, that surprise, and that make customers feel valued and special. In an age where there are so many options available, what differentiates a successful brand from the rest is its ability to create unforgettable moments that generate loyalty and a genuine bond with its audience.

The first step to creating an experience that enchants is to know your customers well. You can't enchant someone without understanding what they like, what they care about, or what they need. This involves listening to your customers, analyzing their behaviors, and having a clear understanding of their expectations. Once you know who they are and what they value, you can tailor each interaction to make them feel like the experience is tailor-made for them. For example, if you run a clothing business and you know that your customers like sustainable fashion, you can highlight how your products are made from eco-friendly materials and highlight the positive impact they have on the environment. This way, you won't just be selling a product, but offering an experience that aligns with your audience's values.

An important part of creating an experience that people love is being consistent with your brand values. If your customers feel that there is authenticity behind what you offer, they will be more inclined to trust you and feel connected to your brand. This means that every touchpoint with your customer should reflect the values that you stand for. From the design of your product to the way you communicate on social media or in customer service, everything should be consistent. If your brand focuses on simplicity and minimalism, make sure that your messaging is clear and direct, and that the shopping experience is as easy as possible. By being consistent, you will create a seamless and enjoyable experience that will make customers feel understood and valued.

Another key aspect of making your customers fall in love is surprising them. People appreciate surprises, especially when they are positive and go beyond what they expected. These surprises can be small, but they have a big impact. For example, you could send a personalized note with each purchase or include a small extra gift that customers weren't expecting. Another way to surprise your customers is to provide faster service than promised or follow up after the purchase to make sure they are satisfied. Small attentions and unexpected gestures are what make a brand stand out and make customers want to come back again and again.

Personalization is another key to creating an experience that delights. Today, consumers expect brands to speak to them in a personalized way, to understand their preferences, and to offer products or services tailored to their individual needs. Technology makes personalization much easier, as it allows you to collect data about your customers and use it to offer targeted recommendations. For example, if you run an online store, you can personalize the shopping experience by suggesting products based on your customers' previous purchases or items they've recently viewed. The more personalized the experience, the more likely customers are to feel that the brand knows and understands them, which strengthens the emotional bond and increases loyalty.

Customer service also plays a key role in creating an experience that people love. It doesn't matter how good your product is if your customer service is poor or inattentive. Customers want to feel heard and supported when they have a problem or question. Therefore, it's essential to offer high-quality customer service that is fast, efficient and friendly. Responding to customer queries promptly, resolving problems effectively and treating each person with respect and kindness are factors that make a big difference. If you make your customers feel that you really care about their satisfaction, they will be much more inclined to continue buying from your brand and recommend it to others.

Another way to create a memorable experience is to offer added value in every interaction. This doesn't necessarily mean giving out discounts or freebies, but rather offering something that is useful, entertaining, or inspiring to your customers. This could be exclusive content, such as tutorials, guides, or behind-the-scenes videos that show how your products are made. You can also host special events, either online or in-person, where customers can learn more about your brand or interact with your team. By continually providing value beyond the product or service you sell, you'll be building a deeper, more meaningful relationship with your audience.

Customer experience should also be easy and frictionless. In a world where people value their time more and more, offering a seamless and hassle-free experience is essential to win over customers. From the purchasing process to after-sales service, everything should be as simple as possible. If you have an online store, make sure it's easy to navigate, the checkout process is fast, and delivery is efficient. If customers have to go through a lot of complicated steps to purchase your product or resolve a problem, they're likely to get frustrated and look elsewhere. By making the experience as convenient as possible, you'll be making it easier for customers to enjoy every interaction with your brand.

Transparency and honesty are also key elements to creating an experience that customers love. Customers value brands that are transparent and communicate clearly. If you make a mistake, it's important to admit it and resolve it quickly and effectively. People understand that mistakes happen, but it's how you deal with them that really makes the difference. Being honest with your customers, being human, and always looking to improve the experience will show that you care about their satisfaction. Transparency builds trust, and when customers trust your brand, they're more likely to feel emotionally connected to you and continue to choose you.

Creating an experience your customers love also means thinking about the little details. It's those subtle touches that often make the difference. It can be something as simple as your product packaging, the design of your website, or the tone of your social media messages. Small details show that you care about your customers' entire experience, not just the transaction. Pretty packaging or a thank you email after a purchase may seem like a small thing, but those details are what often leave a lasting impression and get customers talking about your brand to their friends and family.

In short, creating an experience that your customers love requires a customer-centric approach, with a deep understanding of their needs and desires. It involves offering personalized service, surprising with small gestures, being consistent with your brand values, and providing value in every interaction. It's also important to make the experience as simple as possible, be transparent at all times, and pay attention to the small details. When you manage to create an experience that touches your customers' emotions, you'll not only win sales, but you'll be building long-term relationships that will make people come back again and again, and become true ambassadors for your brand.

The Power of Storytelling in your Brand

Storytelling is one of the most powerful tools a brand can use to connect with its audience. Throughout history, people have told stories to convey knowledge, values, and emotions. Stories have the ability to capture our attention, make us feel part of something bigger, and generate deep connections. Applying this technique to your brand can make a big difference, as it allows you to humanize your business, making it more approachable and memorable for those who discover it.

The power of storytelling for your brand lies in its ability to generate an emotional connection with your customers. People don't just buy products for what they are, but for what they mean. When you buy a pair of sneakers from a well-known brand, you're not just buying the shoes, but also the idea of belonging to a group, adopting a lifestyle, or expressing certain values. Stories help convey those ideas more powerfully than any list of features or benefits. A well-told story can make a customer identify with your brand in a deeper way, creating a bond that goes beyond a simple transaction.

Telling your brand's story doesn't just mean talking about when and where it was founded, or the products you offer. It's about sharing what's behind it, why you exist, the values that drive you, and the challenges you've overcome. Consumers like to know that there are real people behind a brand, with dreams, goals, and struggles. This makes your brand more authentic and allows customers to feel like they're not just buying a product, but supporting a cause or being part of something more meaningful.

One of the keys to storytelling is authenticity. The stories that really resonate are those that are genuine, that reflect the truth behind your brand. You don't have to come up with a grandiose or exaggerated narrative; the important thing is that it's honest. People have a very keen radar for what's fake or forced, so it's always better to be authentic. If your story is humble, but told with sincerity, it will be much more effective than a bombastic story that doesn't feel real. Authenticity creates trust, and trust is essential for customers to feel connected to your brand.

Storytelling can also help you differentiate yourself in a crowded market. Nowadays, there are many brands offering similar products or services, and what often makes one stand out from the rest is the story behind it. Imagine you sell coffee. There are thousands of coffee brands on the market, but if you can tell the story of how your coffee comes from small farmers who care for the land and practice sustainable methods, or how each bean is carefully selected to ensure the best quality, you are adding value that goes beyond the product itself. Suddenly, your coffee is not just a drink, but an experience that has meaning, and that is something that many people will be willing to pay for.

Another important aspect of storytelling is that it allows you to create a narrative around the customer experience. Successful brands don't just tell their story, they invite their customers to be a part of it. This can be achieved in many ways, such as sharing testimonials from satisfied customers, showing how your products have improved people's lives, or even inviting your customers to tell their own stories in relation to your brand. When people feel like they are part of a brand's story, their loyalty increases considerably, as they feel more emotionally connected.

The power of storytelling also extends to how you present your products. Simply listing the technical features of a product is not the same as telling the story of how it was created, what inspired its design, or how it has been tested in extreme conditions to ensure its quality. A well-told story can make something as simple as a rain jacket become a symbol of adventure and endurance. This is a strategy that many successful brands have used: they don't sell products, they sell experiences and emotions.

Emotions are at the heart of storytelling. When you tell a story that touches people's emotions, they are more likely to remember your brand and feel more inclined to choose you over the competition. Emotions like joy, surprise, nostalgia or even sadness can be very powerful if used in the right way. It's not about manipulating people, but about showing the human side of your brand and allowing your customers to feel that there is something deeper behind what you are offering.

An interesting aspect of storytelling is that it can evolve over time. As your brand grows and faces new challenges, you can continue to tell new stories. Success stories, difficulties overcome, key moments in your brand's history are all opportunities to continue connecting with your audience. People enjoy seeing the evolution of something they believe in, and when you share important milestones of your brand with your audience, you're allowing them to be part of that journey.

Additionally, the stories you tell don't always have to be about your brand. You can also tell stories that speak to the values your company stands for or the issues that are important to your audience. For example, if your brand promotes a healthy lifestyle, you can share inspiring stories of people who have transformed their lives through healthy habits. These stories not only reinforce your brand message, but they also offer value to your audience, which in turn strengthens the relationship they have with you.

The medium in which you tell your story also matters. Today, brands have many platforms to tell their stories, from social media to blogs and videos. Each platform has its own style and format, and it's important to tailor your story to each one. A short, emotional video on Instagram can grab people's attention in a way that a long text wouldn't, while a detailed blog can be a great way to dig deeper into your brand's story for those who want to know more. Leveraging these platforms creatively will allow you to reach different types of audiences and keep your story fresh and relevant.

Finally, storytelling is a tool that can also create a positive social impact. If your brand is committed to a social or environmental cause, telling the story of how you are contributing to that cause can inspire your customers and make them feel proud to support your business. Brands that are seen as agents of positive change in the world usually have much more loyal followers, as people want to feel part of something bigger than themselves.

In short, storytelling has immense power to build an emotional connection, differentiate your brand, and create a loyal community. Telling your brand story, being authentic, emotional, and consistent in your narrative are key factors in engaging your audience and making them identify with you. When people feel like they are buying not just a product, but also a story they can relate to, they are more likely to become loyal customers and long-term advocates of your brand.

Humanizing your Personal Brand

Humanizing your personal brand is a crucial step to authentically connect with your audience and differentiate yourself in an increasingly competitive world. A humanized personal brand is not just about showing what you do or selling what you offer, but about sharing who you are, what your values are, and how you relate to the people who follow you or buy your products and services. By showing yourself as you are, without artifice or masks, you manage to generate a much deeper connection, since people tend to trust more those they consider authentic and close.

The first step to humanizing your personal brand is to be transparent. Transparency builds trust, and trust is the foundation of any relationship, whether personal or business. You don't have to be perfect or pretend to be. In fact, sharing some of your challenges and failures can make people relate to you. We all face struggles at some point, and when you show vulnerability, you make it clear that you are a real person, just like anyone else. This creates a more sincere connection and makes you seem approachable.

Another way to humanize your personal brand is by sharing your values and beliefs. People are looking to connect with others who share their ideals or worldviews. If honesty, empathy, or sustainability are important to you, don't hesitate to communicate that. Your values are a fundamental part of who you are, and when you communicate them, you attract people who align with those beliefs. Not only does this strengthen your relationship with your audience, but it also helps you create a community that goes beyond a simple business relationship.

Authenticity is key to humanizing your personal brand. Being authentic means being yourself, without trying to be someone you're not or acting according to what you think others expect of you. In a world where many seek to project an image of perfection on social media, being authentic can be a breath of fresh air for your audience. It's not about sharing every detail of your life, but about being consistent with who you are and what you stand for. If you try to project an image that isn't real, sooner or later people will notice, and this can negatively affect the trust they have placed in you.

Storytelling, or telling your story, also plays a big role in humanizing your personal brand. Telling the story of how you got to where you are, the struggles you've faced, and the lessons you've learned along the way can be very powerful. People love stories because they help us understand and connect with others. When you share your story, you offer your audience a deeper insight into who you are and what drives you. Not only does this make you more human, but it also allows people to feel closer to you and therefore more inclined to support you.

Genuine interaction with your audience is another way to humanize your personal brand. Instead of treating people as just numbers or followers, it's important to see them as human beings with their own needs, questions, and concerns. Responding to their messages, comments, or emails in an authentic and personalized way can make a huge difference. This shows that you value the people who follow you and that you're willing to take the time to interact with them. In the long run, this strengthens the relationship and makes your audience feel more connected to you.

Showing the "behind the scenes" of your life or business is also an effective strategy to humanize your personal brand. People often see the end result, but rarely have the opportunity to learn about the process behind it. Sharing how you work, the challenges you face in your day-to-day life, or even more relaxed moments of your personal life, makes you more relatable. These more spontaneous and authentic moments allow your audience to see the more human and real side of your brand. You don't have to share everything, but showing small snippets of your life can be enough to create a stronger bond.

The language you use is also important to humanize your personal brand. Speaking in a clear, accessible, and friendly way makes people feel more comfortable with you. Avoid excessive use of technical jargon or an overly formal tone, unless your audience requires it. Instead, seek to communicate as you would with a close friend, with naturalness and empathy. The more human your way of speaking and interacting is, the easier it will be for people to identify with you.

It's important to remember that humanizing your personal brand isn't just about showing your positive side or moments of success, but also about sharing the challenges and obstacles you face. Life isn't perfect, and when you show the tough times, you convey that you're a real person who also struggles. Not only does this make you more relatable, but it can also inspire others who are going through similar situations. Seeing how you deal with hardships and keep moving forward can be a source of motivation for your audience.

Additionally, involving your community in the process is another powerful way to humanize your brand. You can ask your followers for opinions, ideas, or suggestions on topics that interest you or that are related to your brand. Making people feel heard and valued strengthens the relationship and creates a sense of belonging. When followers feel like they are part of something bigger and have a voice, they feel more engaged with your personal brand.

Another way to humanize your personal brand is to collaborate with other people or brands that share your values. Collaborations can show a different side of your personality and expand your reach to new audiences, but more importantly, they reflect your ability to work as a team and share your successes with others. These partnerships can also lead to new stories and experiences that you can share with your audience, adding more layers to the humanization of your brand.

Finally, to humanize your personal brand, it is essential to maintain consistency between what you say and what you do. If you talk about the importance of empathy, but then fail to practice it in your interactions, people will notice that incongruity. Actions speak louder than words, and a humanized personal brand must be supported by behaviors that reinforce the values and principles you promote. Consistency in how you present yourself to the world, in all aspects of your professional and personal life, reinforces the credibility and strength of your brand.

In short, humanizing your personal brand involves being transparent, authentic, accessible, and consistent in every aspect of your interaction with others. By sharing your values, telling your story, genuinely engaging with your audience, and showing the process behind what you do, you create a deeper, longer-lasting connection with people. Personal brands that become humanized have the ability to stand out in a world full of competition, because they don't just focus on selling, but on creating meaningful relationships with those who follow them.

Evelyn Wright

From Local to Global

Going from local to global is a dream come true for many brands. It's the moment when a company or personal brand transcends geographic boundaries and reaches audiences in different parts of the world. In the digital age we live in, this process is more accessible than ever, as the internet has broken down many of the barriers that previously limited brands to their geographic area. However, making this leap isn't just about selling to more people; it's about adapting to different cultures, understanding new markets, and maintaining the essence of your brand while growing on a global scale.

The first step in taking a brand from local to global is to understand your own local market. It's crucial to know what makes your brand successful in the context where it started. What do people appreciate about you? What products or services sell the most? What values or characteristics best represent your brand? By understanding this, you can identify which aspects of your brand need to remain constant as you expand your reach. Consistency is key; brands that manage to grow globally do so without losing sight of what made them unique in the first place.

Once you have a good understanding of your local market, the next step is to do detailed research on the international markets you are interested in. Each country and region has its own preferences, behaviours and consumer customs. What works in one place may not be as successful in another, so it is essential to know the particularities of the market you want to enter. What are the consumer trends? How is the competition behaving? What products or services are most in demand? These questions are essential to making informed decisions about how to adapt your brand to the new market.

Language is a crucial aspect to consider when you want to expand from local to global. Although English is a widely used language in international business, not all people speak or understand it fluently. Depending on the markets you target, you will likely need to translate not only your products, but also your content and marketing messages. However, it's not just about literal translation; you need to make sure that the cultural adaptation is accurate. Words and phrases that are common in one country may not have the same impact in another, or may even be misinterpreted. It's important to have localization experts who can help you make sure that your message remains clear and effective in any language.

Another important aspect of global expansion is marketing and advertising. The strategy you use to promote your brand locally may not be as effective in international markets. Social media platforms, marketing trends, and consumer habits vary from country to country. For example, while Facebook and YouTube are global platforms, in some countries like China, local social media like WeChat or Weibo are more relevant. Adapting your marketing strategy to local platforms and preferences can make a huge difference in how your brand is received in new markets.

Logistics is another major challenge when taking a brand from local to global. You need to make sure your product can be delivered efficiently and cost-effectively across different countries. This involves not only working with good suppliers and shipping systems, but also understanding local laws and regulations regarding import and export. In some cases, you may need to adjust your packaging or labeling to meet the standards of a particular country. It's also crucial to consider delivery times and customer expectations. Consumers in different countries may have different expectations as to how long they're willing to wait for a product, so it's important to adjust your processes to meet those expectations.

One issue that can't be ignored when we talk about going from local to global is culture. Every country has its own cultural identity, and what may be a successful product or marketing message in one country may not resonate in another due to cultural differences. It's crucial to take into account the customs, beliefs, and values of the new markets you're targeting. If you manage to adapt your brand in a respectful and appropriate way to the local culture, you have a better chance of generating a deeper connection with the public. On the other hand, if you don't pay attention to these details, you could make mistakes that damage your reputation and alienate you from consumers.

However, expanding a brand globally doesn't mean you have to give up your local identity. The most successful brands are those that manage to find a balance between maintaining their essence and adapting to different markets. A great example of this is how some fast food brands have adjusted their menus in different countries to respect local food traditions, while also keeping some of their signature products that make them recognizable around the world. This hybrid approach, mixing the global with the local, allows brands to feel close and relevant to a wider audience.

Technology also plays a key role in global expansion. E-commerce platforms, social media, and digital marketing tools allow even small local brands to reach a global audience without needing physical infrastructure in each country. These tools make it easier to manage operations remotely, communicate with international customers, and sell products in multiple markets. Leveraging technology efficiently can be a huge competitive advantage for brands looking to expand beyond their borders.

Another aspect to consider is customer service. When your brand goes global, it's important to be able to offer customer support in different languages and time zones. Consumers value a seamless and accessible experience, so having a customer service team that can answer questions and resolve issues quickly and efficiently is key to maintaining a good reputation overseas. Many brands choose to use chatbots or automated customer services, but it's essential that these systems work well in all the languages you speak and offer helpful answers.

Global expansion can also bring with it new financial challenges. The costs of operating in different countries, international taxes, shipping fees, and exchange rate changes are all factors that can affect your profit margin. It's important to work with a financial team that has experience in international operations and can help you manage these challenges effectively. Proper planning and budgeting is essential to ensure your expansion is profitable and sustainable over time.

Finally, taking your brand from local to global is a gradual process. You don't need to expand to many countries at once. In fact, it's more advisable to start with nearby or easier-to-penetrate markets before moving on to those that are more challenging. As you gain experience in managing international markets, you can expand your reach in a more secure and controlled manner. The key is to be patient, adapt to changes, and always be willing to learn from each new challenge.

In conclusion, expanding a brand from local to global is both an exciting and challenging opportunity. It involves adapting your marketing strategy, learning about new markets, adjusting your logistics processes, and maintaining consistency in your identity. However, with proper planning, an open mindset, and a willingness to learn and adapt, it is possible to take your brand beyond its original borders and turn it into a brand with global impact.

Collaborations and Brand Ambassadors

Brand partnerships and brand ambassadorships are two of the most powerful strategies you can use to strengthen your brand and increase its visibility. In a world where competition is increasing and consumers are bombarded with information, finding authentic and effective ways to connect with your audience is essential. Brand partnerships and brand ambassadorships allow you to reach new audiences, strengthen your brand's credibility, and create a closer bond with consumers.

Let's start with collaborations. Collaborating with other brands, companies, or individuals can be a great way to expand your reach and attract new customers. Collaborations don't have to be complicated or expensive, but they do need to be strategic. It's important that you choose partners who share the same values or who complement what you offer. For example, if you have a clothing brand, you could collaborate with an accessories brand that has a similar audience, but offers different products than yours. This way, you both gain exposure to new audiences, without either of you seeing the other as competition.

Collaborations can take many forms. One of the most common is co-branding, where two brands come together to create a unique product or service that combines the best of both. Not only does this generate interest among consumers, but it also adds value to what each brand offers. A good example of this is collaborations between technology and fashion brands, where the design of a product bears the signature of both companies, creating an attractive item for fans of both brands. However, collaborations are not limited to just products; they can also include joint events, advertising campaigns or content shared on social media.

The success of a collaboration depends heavily on the alignment between the brands. If the brands have completely different target audiences or conflicting values, the collaboration may not resonate well. It is essential that there is consistency and that both parties benefit from each other. Successful collaborations create a synergy where the sum is greater than the parts. In other words, the collaboration brings more value than if both brands had acted separately. Therefore, you should carefully choose who you partner with and what type of collaboration makes the most sense for your brand.

On the other hand, brand ambassadors are another effective way to create a closer bond between your brand and your consumers. Brand ambassadors are people who represent your brand in a positive light and help promote it to their own audience. These ambassadors can be public figures, influencers, or even ordinary customers who love your brand and are willing to share their experience with others. The key is that the brand ambassador is authentic and credible, and that their relationship with your brand is not perceived as purely commercial.

Choosing a good brand ambassador means finding someone who really connects with your company's values. It's not just about choosing the most famous person or the one with the most followers on social media, but about selecting someone who really uses and appreciates your products or services. When a brand ambassador speaks about your company from their own experience, the people who follow them perceive that message as more genuine and trustworthy. This is crucial in an environment where traditional advertising is often ignored or viewed with skepticism.

The job of a brand ambassador can vary depending on the strategy you choose. Some brand ambassadors focus on creating content for social media, sharing posts or videos where they use your products. Others may participate in brand events or advertising campaigns. It's also common for brand ambassadors to generate reviews or testimonials that you can then share on your website or digital platforms. The most important thing is that their participation always feels natural and aligned with your brand image.

One of the advantages of working with brand ambassadors is that they often have a closer and more direct relationship with their followers than large companies. Consumers tend to trust recommendations from people they consider peers or role models, which makes the message reach more effectively. When a brand ambassador speaks positively about a product, people are more inclined to try it because it comes from someone they trust.

In addition, the ambassador is usually in constant contact with their audience, which allows the promotion of your brand to be continuous and not just on a one-time basis.

It's important to note that the success of a brand ambassador relationship depends on it being a mutually beneficial relationship. It's not just about the ambassador speaking highly of your brand; you also need to provide value to him or her. This can be in the form of free products, financial compensation, or even exclusive access to events or launches. Ideally, both parties will feel motivated to work together and the relationship will be sustainable in the long term.

In addition to influencers or public figures, you can also consider your own customers as brand ambassadors. Sometimes, the best advocates for your brand are those people who already use your brand and love your products. These people, while they may not have thousands of followers on social media, can be incredibly valuable because their recommendations are often seen as the most sincere and authentic. Fostering close relationships with your customers and encouraging them to share their experiences can be a powerful strategy to turn them into brand ambassadors. Rewards programs or special discounts can encourage them to talk more about your brand among their friends and family.

Measuring the impact of brand ambassadorships and collaborations is essential. It is not enough to launch a campaign and expect results; it is important to monitor performance and evaluate how effective the collaboration has been. Metrics such as increased web traffic, growth of followers on social networks or an increase in sales can give you an idea of how effective the collaboration or the work of the ambassadors has been. This way, you can adjust your strategy for future collaborations or relationships with brand ambassadors.

In conclusion, both brand partnerships and brand ambassadors are powerful tools to grow your business and authentically connect with your audience. Partnerships allow two brands to join forces to reach new audiences, while brand ambassadors help build a more personal and closer connection with consumers. The key is to choose strategic partners who share your values and to maintain an authentic relationship with the ambassadors so that their support for your brand is genuine. If you manage to do it right, these strategies can help take your brand to a new level of success and recognition.

Measuring and Optimizing Your Brand's Success

Measuring and optimizing your brand's success is a crucial part of ensuring your business continues to grow steadily and effectively. While it may seem complicated at first, understanding how to evaluate your brand's performance is simpler than it seems. At its core, it's about analyzing what's working, what's not, and adjusting your strategy based on the results. In this chapter, we'll explore how to measure a brand's success and how to make adjustments to improve its performance over time.

The first step to measuring your brand's success is to clearly define what "success" means to you. Brand success can mean different things depending on your goals. For some brands, success might be an increase in sales or a larger market share. For others, it might mean increased brand recognition, improved public perception, or increased customer loyalty. So before you measure anything, it's important to set clear, specific goals. Do you want to increase your social media following? Do you want more people to buy your product online? Or would you like to improve customer satisfaction? Defining these goals will give you a clear guide on what aspects of your brand you should measure.

Once you have your goals clear, the next step is to identify the key performance indicators (KPIs) that will allow you to measure the success of your brand. KPIs are metrics that help you evaluate whether you are achieving your goals. Some of the most common KPIs include growth in the number of followers on social media, traffic to your website, sales conversions, customer retention rate, and customer satisfaction level. For example, if your goal is to increase brand awareness, one of your KPIs could be the number of mentions or interactions on social media. If your goal is to improve sales, a key KPI could be the number of sales generated through specific marketing campaigns.

Social media is one of the most powerful tools for measuring a brand's success. Platforms like Facebook, Instagram, and Twitter offer a wealth of data that can help you understand how your audience is interacting with your brand. You can analyze metrics like the number of likes, comments, shares, and followers. These metrics give you an idea of how much interest your brand is generating among your target audience. Additionally, many of these platforms offer analytics tools that allow you to see in detail what types of posts are generating the most engagement and which ones aren't performing as well. This allows you to adjust your content and social media strategy to improve results.

Another important aspect of measuring your brand's success is web traffic. Your website is the hub of your online presence, and understanding how users interact with it can provide you with a wealth of valuable insights. Tools like Google Analytics allow you to measure how many people visit your site, how much time they spend on it, what pages they visit, and where they're coming from. If you see that traffic to your site is increasing, that's a sign that your brand is generating interest. But if people visit your site and quickly leave without taking any action (like making a purchase or signing up for your newsletter), then it may be a sign that you need to optimize your website or adjust your messaging.

Customer satisfaction surveys are another powerful way to measure your brand's success. Directly asking your customers what they think of your products or services allows you to get valuable feedback that can help you improve. You can do surveys via email, on your website, or even on social media. Ask your customers if they are satisfied with what you offer, what improvements they would like to see, and how they would describe their overall experience with your brand. The key is to ask open-ended questions and be willing to receive both criticism and praise. Criticism, while sometimes difficult to hear, is an opportunity to improve and adjust what isn't working.

Customer retention rate is one of the most important indicators for measuring the long-term success of your brand. Getting new customers is important, but retaining the ones you already have is key to building a strong brand. Customer retention measures how many people continue to buy from you or use your services after the first time. If you find that many of your customers aren't returning, you may need to look at what aspects of your brand or service need tweaking. Maybe you need to improve customer service, offer loyalty programs, or simply communicate more effectively with them.

Once you've gathered all of this data, the next step is to optimize. Optimizing means making adjustments and improvements based on the information you've gathered. If you notice that certain social media posts are more successful than others, you can start focusing more on that type of content. If you find that certain pages on your website aren't driving conversions, you may need to reconsider the design or information you present on those pages. The key to optimization is to always be willing to make changes and experiment with new ideas.

Another important aspect of optimization is A/B testing. A/B testing is a technique where you create two different versions of a marketing campaign, web page, or ad and test them to see which one performs better. For example, you could test two different headlines for a social media ad and see which one generates more clicks. Or you could test two versions of a landing page on your website to see which one converts more visitors into customers. A/B testing allows you to make decisions based on data and not just assumptions, which increases the likelihood of success.

Brand optimization isn't a one-time thing; it's an ongoing process. The market is constantly changing, and consumer preferences evolve over time, too. That's why it's important to regularly review and adjust your brand strategy based on the results you're getting. Stay on top of new trends, observe what your competitors are doing, and always listen to your customers. This will help you keep your brand fresh and relevant in an ever-changing environment.

Also, don't forget to measure and optimize not only the external aspects of your brand, such as advertising and content, but also the internal aspects. Evaluate how your marketing team is performing, whether the tools you use are adequate, and whether your internal processes are efficient. Sometimes, improving internal efficiency can have a direct positive impact on the success of your brand, as it allows everything to run more smoothly and quickly.

Finally, it's important to remember that measuring your brand's success isn't just about numbers. While metrics are helpful, you should also consider the qualitative aspect of your brand. What do people think about your brand? What emotions does it generate? Sometimes, a single satisfied customer can be more valuable than a thousand social media followers if that customer is so impressed with your brand that they become a loyal advocate. Personal success stories, positive reviews, and strong customer relationships are all signs that your brand is making a positive impact—something that often can't be measured by statistics alone.

In short, measuring and optimizing your brand's success is an ongoing process that involves defining clear goals, monitoring key metrics, and making strategic adjustments to constantly improve. From social media analytics and web traffic to customer satisfaction surveys and retention, there are many ways to gain valuable insights into how your brand is performing. The key is to be proactive, willing to learn, and always be ready to make changes to take your brand to the next level.

Make People Love Buying Your Brand

Getting people to love buying your brand is undoubtedly the most desired goal for any entrepreneur or business. It's not just about selling a product or service; it's about creating an emotional connection between your brand and your customers. Getting a person to prefer your brand over others, even when they have plenty of options, requires a careful strategy that goes beyond a simple business transaction. Here we'll explore how you can get people to not only buy your brand, but fall in love with it, leading to long-term loyalty.

The first step to getting people to love buying from your brand is to make sure they understand the value you offer. It's critical that your brand is presented as more than just a product or service. You need to show how your brand improves people's lives or solves an important problem. People don't buy products, they buy solutions, they buy experiences. For example, if you sell clothing, you're not just offering fabric and stitching; you're offering style, confidence, and a way to express yourself. If you sell technology, you're not just offering electronics, you're offering the ability to simplify and improve people's everyday lives. Communicating this value clearly and directly is essential to making customers feel like they're making the right choice by buying from you.

Another key factor in making people love buying from your brand is the shopping experience. This is a point that many companies overlook, but it is crucial to creating a positive customer relationship. The shopping experience encompasses everything from how customers find your brand, to the moment they receive the product and beyond. An easy-to-navigate website, a simple and fast checkout process, friendly and efficient customer service, and on-time shipping are just a few of the aspects that can make all the difference. If you make shopping easy and hassle-free, customers are more likely to return. People appreciate brands that take care of all the details and make the experience seamless and enjoyable.

An important part of getting people to love buying from your brand is creating a relationship based on trust. Trust is built by being consistent, delivering on the promises you make, and offering a quality product or service. If a customer trusts that your brand will always deliver, they will be much more willing to buy from you again and again. To build that trust, it's vital to be transparent in all aspects of your business. This includes being honest about what your product can do, offering clear guarantees, and being accessible if there are any issues. Customers value honesty and prefer brands that don't try to sell you something they're not.

Customer service is another critical aspect of making people love buying from your brand. While many people associate customer service with problem-solving, it actually goes much further than that. Exceptional customer service can turn an ordinary shopping experience into a memorable one. Responding quickly to queries, resolving any issues efficiently and with a positive attitude, and showing genuine interest in your customers' needs are all actions that show that you care about every person who purchases from your brand. When customers feel that they are valued, they are more inclined to return and recommend your brand to others.

It's also important to personalize the shopping experience as much as possible. Personalization is one of the most effective strategies for making customers feel a deeper connection with your brand. This can be something as simple as remembering a customer's name or their previous preferences, or it can be as sophisticated as sending personalized recommendations based on their past purchases. When people feel like your brand "knows" them, they're more likely to develop an emotional attachment and enjoy the experience of shopping at your store. Personalization makes them feel like they're not just another number on your customer list, but that they're important to you.

Another powerful strategy to get people to love buying your brand is to build a community around it. People tend to gravitate toward brands that stand for something bigger than the product itself. Whether it's a social cause, a lifestyle, or a set of shared values, building a community around your brand strengthens your relationship with customers. You can do this through social media, events, or even loyalty programs that reward customers for their loyalty. When people feel like they're a part of something, they don't just buy your brand for what you sell, but for what you stand for.

One element that we cannot ignore when we talk about making people love buying from your brand is the emotional aspect. Brands that manage to establish an emotional bond with their customers are the ones that are most successful in the long term. This emotional bond can be created in many ways, such as telling an authentic story behind the creation of your brand, showing empathy for your customers' needs, or getting involved in causes that are important to your audience. Emotions are powerful, and when you manage to make your brand evoke positive feelings, customers not only buy because they need the product, but because it makes them feel good.

Consistency also plays a key role in this process. You can't expect people to love your brand if the experience you offer is inconsistent. Every touchpoint with your brand should reflect the same values and quality. From your website to your social media, to the packaging and presentation of your products, everything should be aligned with the image you want to project. If customers know what to expect from your brand and always receive what they expected or more, they are much more likely to develop a lasting attachment and loyalty.

Last but not least, you should constantly seek to exceed your customers' expectations. It's in the small details where you can surprise and delight your customers. Fast shipping, products that exceed expectations in quality, and unexpected surprises (like a thank you note or a small gift) are simple yet effective ways to make people feel special. When you exceed their expectations, you don't just earn a sale, you earn a loyal customer who will speak positively of your brand and come back again and again.

In short, getting people to love buying from your brand is a process that requires time, effort, and a well-thought-out strategy. You need to offer value, provide an exceptional shopping experience, build trust, and establish an emotional connection with your customers. In addition, it is essential to be consistent and personalize the experience as much as possible. If you manage to apply these principles, you will be on the right path to not only sell products or services, but to create a brand that people truly love and want to continue interacting with over time.